The Media

by
Belinda Hollyer
Illustrated by Jacky Fleming

couch potato

couch potato

h
Hodder
Children's
Books

a division of Hodder Headline plc

Edited by Vic Parker

Layout by Joy Mutter

Published by Hodder Children's Books 1998

10 9 8 7 6 5 4 3 2 1

ISBN 0 340 72291 6

A Catalogue record for this book is available from the
British Library.

Printed and bound by The Guernsey Press Co. Ltd.,
Guernsey, Channel Islands

Hodder Children's Books
A division of Hodder Headline plc
338 Euston Road
London NW1 3BH

Contents

SO WHAT IS 'THE MEDIA'?

The media is the term people use for the collection of communication channels in the modern world. You connect with these channels every time you switch on a television set, or listen to the radio or a CD, or read a magazine or a newspaper.

The media are an immensely powerful force. They bombard almost everyone on Earth with messages and send them into space, too. They use every communication tool that's available.

oh, sorry, I seem to have got the wrong number . . . .

The media are in most of the rooms in your house ...

... in your living room, kitchen and bedroom; probably even your bathroom. And they're in shops, cinemas, schools and libraries. The media travel with you in cars, buses, planes and ships. You really can't escape them, even if you tried.

As you can see, the channels of communication that make up the media are ones you know well. You use many of them every day. They include television, radio, films and videos, newspapers, magazines, books, and computers. Each one of these is a **medium** of communication (so media is a plural word, not a singular one).

I'm a medium too

You are probably so accustomed to using the media, you don't even think about them. But do you know how much time you spend each week in contact with these channels? Try keeping a media diary to check how much you watch TV and videos, listen to tapes and CDs and the radio, read magazines and newspapers, play computer games, or surf the Internet. You might be surprised to discover just how important the media are in your life.

Yes, our camera crew could be at YOUR front door RIGHT NOW

It's an evil monster!

The modern media are such a powerful force in our lives, that many people fear their influence is bad – especially the influence of television. For example, since TV broadcasts began in the 1950s, there have been thousands of studies of the effects of TV violence. Many people believe that if children watch violent acts on TV, they will not only become accustomed to violence, but also become violent in their own behaviour.

In 1996 a Broadcasting Standards Commission report called <u>Young People and the Media</u> found that 42% of the 10-to-16-year-olds they interviewed had seen <u>Pulp Fiction</u>, even though the film has an R18 certificate. The children had seen the film on video or on Sky TV. A child interviewed for the report said, 'Drugs are drummed into your head like they are bad. But not violence.' The report's author concluded that, 'Videos cannot create aggressive people, but they will make aggressive people commit violent acts more frequently.'

Another concern is simply the
amount of TV that people watch,
instead of doing active things like
playing sport. Critics of the
media claim that people who just
sit passively for hours on end
watching whatever's on the
screen have limited imaginations
and poor concentration spans.
The same things are also claimed
about heavy use of computer
games, videos, and the Internet.

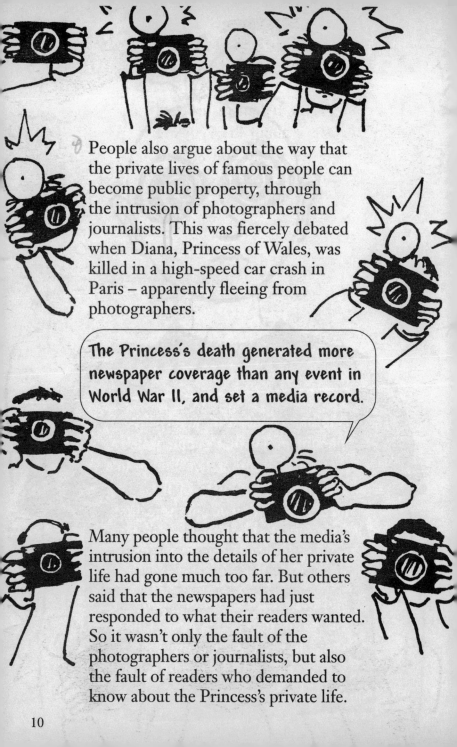

People also argue about the way that the private lives of famous people can become public property, through the intrusion of photographers and journalists. This was fiercely debated when Diana, Princess of Wales, was killed in a high-speed car crash in Paris – apparently fleeing from photographers.

The Princess's death generated more newspaper coverage than any event in World War II, and set a media record.

Many people thought that the media's intrusion into the details of her private life had gone much too far. But others said that the newspapers had just responded to what their readers wanted. So it wasn't only the fault of the photographers or journalists, but also the fault of readers who demanded to know about the Princess's private life.

At the height of her fame, a story about the Princess of Wales would add at least 100,000 copies to the circulation of a tabloid newspaper such as The Mirror or The Sun.

The media themselves – the channels of communication – aren't good or bad. But the uses to which these channels are put – the content of the media channels – can be evaluated, questioned and explored. You can question the choices which are made by the people in charge of the media channels, and the way they convey information.

Stories about crime, disaster and war constitute more than half the news on television.

According to one report, 92% of Americans believe that TV violence contributes to real-life violence.

The media don't create our world. They offer us a picture of it.

There have been more than 3,000 studies of TV violence since the 1950s. All of them seem to agree that heavy watchers of violent TV are more aggressive than light watchers.

Surfing the Internet gives you access to a whole universe of information. No classroom or teacher could offer as much.

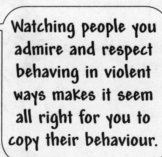

Watching people you admire and respect behaving in violent ways makes it seem all right for you to copy their behaviour.

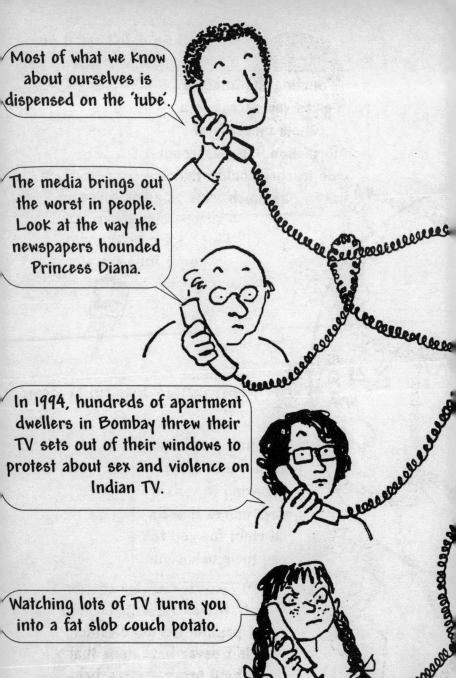

14

Yes, if we didn't see it on TV, it didn't happen.

The tabloids used royal stories as ammunition in a vicious circulation war. But it's the public who bought the papers!

Wasn't that a bit violent of them?

TV coverage of our charity walk helped raise thousands of pounds for the disabled. We'd never have done that without programmers' help.

The media are good at entertaining people and they are also good at teaching them. At their best, they do both at the same time. The visual media (such as film and TV) are famous for being able to show us things that aren't actually present. They can make us see imaginary worlds, or something that's happening right now on the other side of the planet, or even the next door neighbour's budgie collection. That makes them an extraordinarily powerful tool.

hello mum

In Britain, like America, television is the most powerful channel of communication in use. Today, 97% of households have at least one TV set and almost 30% have three or more. We spend more than 40% of our leisure time watching that screen! And in a recent survey, 85% of British people thought TV was the most reliable and accurate source of news reporting. (The rest of Europe thought newspapers were the most reliable and accurate.)

In Britain there are three sorts of TV:

the commercial sector ITV, which is paid for by its advertisers and is broadcast both nationally (Channel 4 and 5) and regionally (on 16 different Channel 3 stations)

the public sector BBC, which is paid for by an annual licence fee and is broadcast nationally

satellite and cable TV, which is paid for by advertisers and by subscriptions, and is broadcast nationally

Digital terrestrial TV will launch in Britain in 1998. There will be 36 channels, divided between the BBC and three commercial sector companies. Digital transmission is more efficient than the present **analogue** system, and it will produce better pictures and sound. The digital signal will be received by the existing roof-top aerials, but you will need to buy a decoder set-top box and pay a subscription. In time, all TV will be transmitted digitally, so this is truly the start of a media revolution.

Read all about it!

Newspapers have been the most powerful medium of communication for about 250 years, but their circulations are now declining in most countries. That isn't just because there are now other, more powerful, media available which can deal more immediately with the news. It is also because newspapers have become less profitable, as advertisers have found other media (like TV) to be more successful. But newspapers are still a very important part of the media scene.

The British buy more newspapers than any other European country, and 66% of the British public read a daily newspaper. Britain also has a comparatively high number of national newspapers, with 11 daily nationals and nine Sunday nationals. Neither the United States nor Canada has any national newspapers at all.

NEWS ON UK NEWSPAPERS

In Britain there are two 'divisions' of newspaper – the **broadsheets** like *The Times* and *The Guardian*, which are printed on large sheets of paper and are more serious than the **tabloids**, which are printed on smaller sheets and often use sensational stories. The 'red top' tabloids like *The Sun* and *The Mirror* are the papers most often accused of intrusive and irresponsible journalism. They are also the ones with the highest circulations (*The Sun* has a circulation of around 4 million, and *The Mirror* around 2.5million). *The Daily Telegraph*, which has the highest broadsheet circulation, has a circulation of only about 1 million.

NEWS EVERY DAY OF THE WEEK

Britain has about a hundred local daily newspapers, as well as more than a thousand weekly ones. And there are many ethnic newspapers too – like *New Nation*, a tabloid paper 'for black people in Britain'.

MORE BAD NEWS!

According to a recent survey, there's 15 times more bad news than good news covered in both national and local papers.

PAPER FOLDS

The last national newspaper to shut down in Britain was *Today* in 1995.

Tuning In

As well as newspapers, the medium of radio is also slowly decreasing in popularity. Even so, in Britain about 85% of people over 15 years of age listen to radio every week – an audience of 40 million people!

Radio broadcasts are divided into four wavebands:

short wave and long wave, which are mostly used for long-distance broadcasts like the World Service and to transmit foreign countries' broadcasts

Commercial radio began in Britain in the 1970s and has since become enormously popular. Now, more than half of British listeners tune in to commercial stations; the rest still listen to one of the BBC's licence-funded stations. Both commercial and BBC radio transmit nationally and locally, and of course they compete with each other for listeners.

medium wave, which is mostly used for local broadcasts

ah... Chopin

and VHF/FM, which is mostly used for national broadcasts.

STOP PRESS STOP PRESS

Digital radio transmissions will be licensed in Britain in 1998, with about 20 new services launching in 1999. These will give you a reception quality as good as a CD, but the decoder receivers will cost several hundred pounds.

There are hundreds of independent radio stations in Britain. Only three broadcast nationally (Classic FM, Virgin and Talk FM) and the rest are regional or local stations. All radio broadcasts must be licensed, even those which are restricted to hospitals or university campuses. Unlicensed (pirate) radio stations can be prosecuted by the Radio Authority, which controls licences.

Make me a star!

The media – particularly TV – presents us with easily-identifiable personalities. For instance, the characters in a TV drama do not have to deal with the boring bits of life. They can control the situations in which they appear and aggressively confront one crisis after another. A character can be dominant, for example, because she is the captain of a star-ship, or because he has a bionic arm. Think of Mickey Mouse and of Sylvester Stallone's 'Rocky'. These characters are media stars.

We're being invaded by intergalactic terrorists. I'll have to mobilise the Special Forces!

When you've done that, Mr Spock, could you pop out for some milk?

Actors, film stars and pop singers used to become celebrities even before TV was invented. But nowadays, through widespread TV exposure, it's even easier to become 'involved' with the lives of famous people and to identify with their strong personalities.

For instance, even the people who present TV programmes often have their private lives written about; they are recognised in the street by fans; they appear on other programmes; they open functions and attend charity events. If there is too much contrast between a star's media personality and what they're like in real life, their fans will be disappointed – even angry.

The behaviour of people who become stars through the media influences the millions of people all over the world who watch and admire them. For instance, when professional sports stars in India were sponsored by a tobacco company, the stars were seen as encouraging young people to smoke. In Britain, tobacco companies will soon be banned from sponsoring sports events.

Media business

Almost all the channels of communication we use are owned by giant corporations which are based in the western world, with global distribution networks. The news, and most of our amusement and entertainment, now comes to us from just a few powerful media empires. The six largest corporations are: Time Warner; Disney; Bertelsmann; Viacom; News International, and Telecommunications Inc. (known as TCI).

Each of the big six companies owns hundreds of newspapers, magazines, book publishers, film studios and TV channels around the world. For example, Time Warner owns Warner Brothers and CNN, as well as many other media companies.

Rupert Murdoch's News International controls 35% of British media, including *The Sun*, *The Times* and *The Sunday Times*, and 40% of BSkyB. And these companies reach a huge audience. For instance, CNN International is transmitted to more than 210 countries and territories worldwide, via a network of 12 satellites. As well as reaching 66 million households in the United States, it also reaches over 78 million households outside it. Similarly, MTV (owned by Viacom) reaches over 250 million homes in 64 countries. It alarms many people that this concentration of media power lies in the hands of so few companies. You can read more about this on pages 104 to 105.

WHERE DID THE MODERN MEDIA COME FROM?

Today's channels of communication are very modern. Most of them have only been in use this century. Your grandparents may have grown up without television. Their parents may have grown up without radio or a telephone. Even newspapers are only a few hundred years old. So what did people do before the invention of the media?

shock.. horror.

scandal

.. fashion tips.

The first forms of communication didn't use any technology. People simply told each other stories. For instance, the myths and legends of Ancient Greece and the Norse sagas were told orally, for tens of hundreds of years, before they were ever written down. All you needed were a great story and an excellent memory. People like Homer, who probably lived around the 10th century BC (that is, almost 3000 years ago) told stories like the Odyssey and the Iliad, which we still know today. Of course, now we have to read them in books, because almost no one in our modern world has a good enough memory to recite the whole of these long stories by heart.

and he HUFFED .. and he PUFFED ..

Most cultures have a similar **oral tradition** of story-telling. The stories remembered and passed down by the bards were the ones that the audiences enjoyed. And you can be sure that the audience's reaction influenced the way in which the stories developed, just as it does now with radio and TV soaps.

Writing it down

The invention of a writing system (around 1400 BC) and the development of writing materials were great technological breakthroughs in communication. Writing allows human communication to be preserved in a permanent form – as long as you have something adequate to write on! But there were problems with early types of paper.

The trouble with papyrus (an early type of paper made from reeds) was because it's easily damaged by water and it's very brittle when it's dry. You therefore have to be extremely careful when you write on it, in case you punch through the surface and tear it. It also cracks and tears if you fold it, so it has to be rolled into scrolls, which made storage and use quite difficult.

don't tell me, the dog ate it.

Parchment was made from animal skin. It lasted
better and was more supple than papyrus, but it
was heavier, more expensive, and
more difficult to obtain
in large quantities.

Paper (made from rags and later also from wood
pulp) was a much better medium. (Now you know
why a newspaper is sometimes called 'the daily
rag'!) Paper could be folded and cut to any size
you needed, and when it was bound in leather or
wood, it lasted well and could be used easily.

The first newspapers in history developed in Roman times. The proceedings of the Roman senate were taken down in note form by a magistrate and then displayed in public, so that the Roman citizens could read them. In this way, citizens could keep in touch with the political issues of their time, much as today we might read about the proceedings of Parliament, or watch them on TV. Roman citizens could find out how certain senators had voted on particular issues, and follow the development of debates and decisions that affected their lives.

Although we call the magistrate's notes an early newspaper (because it was, literally, a piece of paper full of news) it wasn't much like a modern newspaper. The main difference is that there was only one copy! You had to go down to the main town square to read it, because there was no quick or easy way of copying the newspaper. The only method would have been for scribes to write out the news by hand. The fast duplication of written material was still far in the future, as was the printing process.

Printing presses were developed in China in the 11th century. The first ones just used **block printing**, where a whole page of characters and illustrations was carved out of a wooden block and printed as one complete page. That was fine if you just wanted to print the same page, or the same book, over and over again. But it didn't really speed up the process of printing lots of different books.

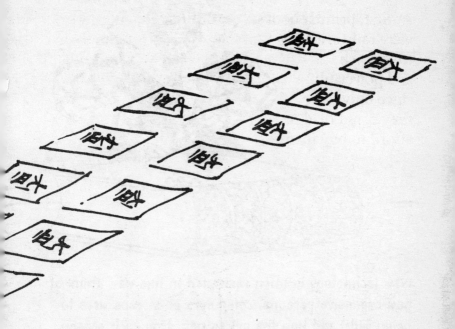

The invention of **moveable type** was a real breakthrough for the development of communications. It was first produced in China and used there for several centuries, but Chinese printers didn't find it a great advantage, because of the complexities of their written language. When moveable type was redeveloped in Germany in the 15th century, printing really began to take off. Pages of printed words could rapidly be assembled and printed, before taking the type apart to form new words on new pages.

The book boom

At first, printed books
were only available
to the rich
and powerful,
since only
they could read or
afford to buy them.

mine

New technology is often restricted in this way. Think of
how expensive personal computers or stereos were to
begin with, and how the prices now drop each season.

But in quite a short time, the printing revolution had
begun to change the way in which people
communicated, in profoundly important ways.
Within 60 years of the invention of moveable type,
there were 1,700 printing presses in Europe,
producing copies of about 40,000 different books. So
information was much more easily available to
people – especially to the rising class of merchants
and city-dwellers, who had enough money to buy a
book and enough education to be able to read it.
Having information available in this new way helped
to change society. Before the spread of printing, it
was a lot easier to control what ordinary people
knew, and so what they thought. But books could
provide different ideas.

At various times throughout history, books have been thought of as dangerous, and access to them – and especially to certain individual titles – has been restricted. Today some governments try to restrict the freedom of the press and of other forms of the media in their countries for exactly the same reason.

The shipping news

The first European newspapers to be the immediate ancestors of our modern ones grew from the private letters of merchants. As merchants travelled between cities and countries, they often wrote to their associates and to other merchants to report on the places they visited and to share information that would be useful in their business.

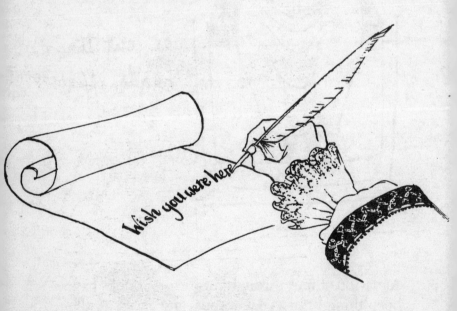

In time, these letters developed into printed leaflets. At least one of these still exists – Lloyd's List, related to the famous insurance house in the City of London.

Lloyd's List began in April 1734, as a single sheet of paper. On one side was printed the prices of stocks and shares, and on the other, a list of shipping movements. It cost three shillings a quarter (that is, about 15p for three month's worth of issues). Merchants and insurance agents came to Lloyd's Coffee House to discuss their business and make deals, and Edward Lloyd, the coffee house owner, started the news-sheet to sell to his clientele.

then we get to the shipping movements

no horoscope?

Daily news

In the 1600s and early 1700s, early British newspapers were often **censored** (see page 94) or closed down, and the publication of home news was sometimes forbidden by law. So pamphlets and broadsheets were produced instead, which were easier to print and distribute. These published mostly gossip and scandal, on single sheets of paper.

(Jokers also called them 'broadsides', the name for the powerful attacking shots fired simultaneously from the line of guns along the side of a ship.) Funnily enough, these days the newspapers that are printed on large sheets of paper – the broadsheets – are the 'respectable' newspapers, while the tabloids – the folded and cut smaller format papers – are the scandal 'rags'.

The first English newspaper was produced in 1665, when the Royal court had fled from London to Oxford, to try to escape the plague. It was produced from time to time to keep the people at court up to date with news of London and Europe, but it lasted only a short while. The first daily English newspaper began in London in 1702, called *The Daily Courant*. But it just re-used stories from other European newspapers. So the news it provided was rather old by the time the European newspapers reached London and were read, translated, re-typeset, printed and distributed. The first genuine daily newspaper was *The Times*, which began in 1785 and is still published.

he didn't!

he did

TECHNOLOGY RULES, OK?

A hundred years ago, today's modern media would have been impossible to imagine or predict. Even Alexander Bell, the inventor of the telephone, thought that only 'every town' would have one in the future. He never dreamed how universal a medium of communication telephones would become in homes and offices, nor that mobile phones would exist, or be so popular.

Although newspapers have been around for more than 200 years they are now considered a dying form of communication. Channels such as radio and TV and the Internet have more popular appeal. The first radio signals were broadcast in 1895, and the first television demonstration was made in 1925, with the first public television service transmitted by the BBC in 1936.

The Internet began as a university communication system between computer users in the 1970s and was further developed as an emergency means of communication in case of nuclear attack. But it was not until the 1990s that an enormous growth in home computer use encouraged its international commercial popularity. Now, you can:

- surf the Net
- visit literally millions of websites or design and launch your own
- send messages to distant friends and business colleagues in just a few seconds
- shop around the world
- use the research facilities of libraries in other towns and countries
- read books
- watch films and listen to music

all from your home-based computer.

It is technology that has made all this possible. The growth of these channels of communication, and of mass access to all forms of the media, is matched only by the development of the technology that underpins it all.

Picture this

We live in the age of television. Viewers are
bombarded by electronic images, in a culture
where what we see drowns out what we hear. If
you watch a TV programme that's 10 or 15 years
old, one thing you're bound to notice is just how
far away the camera is from the people on screen!
Since TV broadcasts began, the camera has
gradually closed in on faces, especially if the
display of emotion is important. A close face-shot
is intimate and engaging.

News stories on TV aren't chosen just because
they are important, or dramatic. They must also
be effective visually. And that's often different
from what makes a good radio, or a good
newspaper, story. A good TV news story has to
show you pictures related to it – and preferably
action film, not still shots.

If the same story is presented in a newspaper, it might not even need a still photo to make the story effective. Words alone can do the job well, but the story will be different because it is told without visual aids.

A radio news item, again told only in words, might take yet another, equally different, perspective – because the words you use to tell a story out loud are different from the ones you use to write it out.

A volcano erupted this morning showering ash for miles around and leaving six people missing, presumed dead . . .

What's the story?

Even within the same medium, news can be reported in different ways. For example, newspapers often take different angles on the same story, each trying to capture the attention and interest of readers. Here is one example, from newspapers at the end of 1997.

Eye transplant from woman with CJD

The risk of organ transplants was highlighted after it was disclosed that eye tissue from a woman was transplanted into three patients before it was discovered she had been suffering from Creutzfeld Jakob disease. Officials said "immediate action" was being taken to improve safety checks, but it was unclear what they might be. **Page 3**

from 'The Mirror',
page 4, 1.12.97

from 'The Independent',
page 1, 1.12.97

PAGE 4   THE MIRROR, Monday, December 1, 1997

PROBE OVER EYE DONOR WITH CJD

By PASCALE PALMER

AN inquiry was under way last night after three patients received transplants from a CJD sufferer.

A woman was found to have had the human form of mad cow disease after dying of lung cancer. But ~~an autopsy report was not passed on to the UK Trans~~ could have been handed

from 'The Guardian',
page 3, 1.12.97

Monday December 1 1997

CJD victim's eyes used in transplants

John Arlidge

THE Government pledged last night to tighten up organ transplant procedures after it was revealed that tissue from a woman suffering from Creutzfeldt-Jakob disease — the human form of mad cow disease — was used in operations on three people.

small hole in our defences here. We'll need to make sure we close it," he said.

A Department of Health spokesman added: "We do not know the full facts but we are making urgent inquiries into how this could have occurred. If there has been a breakdown in communication, we will want to know why. We

HORROR OF DONOR WIFE WHO HAD CJD

from 'The Sun', page 18, 1.12.97

18   THE SUN, Monday, December 1, 1997   3 G

'MAD COW' SHOCK OVER OPS DONOR

By ANDREA BUSFIELD

THREE patients were given eye tissue from a woman suffering from the human form of mad cow disease.

Marion Hamilton, 53, was thought to have died from lung cancer, but a post mortem showed she also had CJD. The findings were not passed to transplant doctors. Eye parts, including her corneas, were then given to two men and a woman in her 80s.

One of Mrs Hamilton's three daughters said in Stirling: "We were never told the post mortem results. These patients could have been handed a death sentence."

She said her mother changed almost overnight

to "a senile old lady," staggering and falling.

The UK Transplant Support Service said: "If we'd known about CJD, we would not have considered transplantation."

Health chiefs in Scotland are investigating.

GREAT DESKAPE

Kayleigh Brocklehurst, eight, was freed at hospital after getting her finger stuck in a hole in her school desk at Halifax, West Yorks.

SUN NEWLYWEDS Jo and Jamie Clary, both 35, put a film of their marriage in Colchester, Essex, on the Internet so friends across the world could see it. **SPOT**

BY NIC FLEMING

THREE patients have received transplants from a CJD victim, it was revealed last night.

Two men and one woman were given eye tissue from Marion Hamilton, a donor card

Service was not notified for more than two months.

Last night, as an urgent investigation was launched, experts

Britain — have not been released. They have not yet been told of the donor's illness and the risks.

Mrs Hamilton, who had three daughters was cared for at

from 'The Express', front page, 1.12.97

Daily Mail, Monday, December 1, 1997

Page 2

CJD shock for transplant patients

Continued from Page One

problem with CJD is that it can be confirmed only after death, by cutting open a patient's brain.

It takes several days for the results to be known — too late for organs such as the heart and liver to be used. Eyes can be stored in liquid nitrogen for up to eight weeks.

Mrs Hamilton's family, from Stirling in Scotland, learned only last week that she was suffering from CJD.

She was admitted to a hospice last December with lung cancer. But she also showed symptoms linked to CJD — the human form of mad cow disease — such as being unsteady on her feet.

Government scientists say the risk of a patient developing CJD

from a donor is low. About one person in 50,000 can be expected to be incubating the 'classic' form of the disease at the time of death, the risk that their organs would be given to someone who then died of CJD is regarded as minimal.

But there is disagreement among experts on the many people who could develop the new strain of CJD in the future from having eaten infected beef.

There is a further problem in that the disease can apparently incubate for several years before it shows.

Dr Helen Grant, a neuropathologist and former senior lecturer at Middlesex Hospital in London, last night played down the risks of infection to the three transplant patients. She said: 'You will not

develop this disease unless you are the right geno-type and only about 30 per cent of the population are.'

Others painted a bleaker picture. Dr Stephen Dealler, a microbiologist at a hospital in the North West of England, said: 'This is horrific. The chance of infection from her tissue is very high. Frankly, it would now be far better for people to die of CJD if they don't die of something else first.'

Richard Lacey, Professor of Microbiology at the University of Leeds and an outspoken critic of the Government's handling of CJD, claimed there was a 'substantial risk' that the three recipients would catch the disease.

About 5,000 people in Britain receive organs each year from

1,900 donors. Some 3,500 receive corneas and the rest receive organs such as hearts.

A spokesman for the UK Transplant Support Service Authority, which acts as a clearing house, said Mrs Hamilton's eyes might have been removed shortly after her death and stored in banks either in Manchester or Bristol. They would then have been transferred to wherever they were needed.

The recipients could be living anywhere in Britain, the said. The surgeons who carried out the transplants had been told last week. She said it was for the patient's doctor to determine whether he or she was a suitable candidate to donate organs.

Asked if the case of Mrs Hamilton had exposed a failure in the

system, she added: 'It would appear so.' Last night, Scottish health minister Sam Galbraith promised to review the system on transplants. He said: 'We will have to try to tighten up procedures.'

'What we really not now to concentrate at centre, is when we explore the possibility in transplantation cases, we consider what are concurrent diseases what possible all that obvious at the time are there. I emphasise that the use of donation of CJD through eye transmission is to be very small.

Mrs Hamilton was separated from her husband Sernaa, but the couple remained close friends.

'She always said that her death would bring someone else's,' he recalled last night. 'It is very sad that what she meant to be a gift has turned out so badly.'

from 'The Daily Mail', page 2, 1.12.97

from 'The Daily Mail', front page, 1.12.97

Inquiry ordered as transplant patients face risk of infection

ORGAN DONOR IN CJD SHOCK

By CHRISTOPHER EVANS and ANNIE BROWN

AN INQUIRY was started last night into why three patients

Council tax

News lite

News programmes, and especially TV news, are cut and edited to fit a very tight schedule. One American news station claims to give their viewers 'all the news in the world in 22 minutes'! For this kind of programming, radio and TV reporters usually need short 'sound-bites' from the people they interview. A **sound-bite** is a quick summary of what someone thinks, in just a few words or a couple of sentences. For such programmes, long or complicated replies to questions don't fit the available time or the expectations of viewers. But if a news item is at all subtle or complicated, a sound-bite summary won't reflect that, and it will probably give only one side of the argument. The constant presentation of simple 'one-liners' in news coverage is called 'dumbing down' the news. This is an accusation often made about TV news programmes and tabloid news coverage.

Political campaigns are so superficial and simplistic. In the 20 seconds we have left, could you tell us why?

Another phrase you often hear connected to news presentation is **spin doctor**. Organisations that are in the news often have their own public relations or media consultant 'spin doctors' who talk to journalists and try to turn the story into a positive one for their side. Politicians, in particular, employ 'spin doctor' press and public relations experts to help them influence public opinion.

NEWS

Because my party's politics ARE simple: honesty, trust, and putting the people's interests first. What more do you need to say?

So how can a reporter select the most important aspects of a news event? Well, suppose that you are the witness to a story, and have to report it.

1: You are walking down the High Street on your way home from school, when you see two men rush out of the newsagent's shop, carrying bags.

2: Life as normal on the High St.

3: The men jump into the van and drive away at high speed.

4: Life as normal on the High St.

5: Then the owner of the newsagent rushes out in the street too, shouting.

You saw everything that happened – or at least, you think you did. But when you tell people about what you saw, you won't give them every detail – that would take far too long. Your listeners would get bored and stop listening before you could get to the best dramatic bits! So you would probably select only these bits for your story:

1: You are walking down the High Street on your way home from school, when you see two men rush out of the newsagent's shop, carrying bags.

2: The men jump into the van and drive away at high speed.

3: Then the owner of the newsagent rushes out in the street too, shouting.

But does your edited story tell the truth?

Well, it might tell the truth as you saw it, but that isn't the only way of looking at the events. It may have looked like a robbery to you, but there are other possibilities.

Perhaps the men ran from the shop for another reason? For instance because they'd seen a traffic warden on the other side of the street and didn't want a parking ticket.

And what were they carrying? Stolen goods – or maybe unsold copies of magazines and newspapers that they were taking back to the distributor?

Maybe the newsagent was shouting because the men had forgotten to take one of the bags?

Down your way

A newspaper editor will consider different people's points of view when deciding which bits of news will be most interesting for its readers.

For instance, a local paper might report international news, but if it does, it will use a local viewpoint. This is mostly because local newspapers are only published weekly or fortnightly, and so any topical international news will be old, or will have changed, by the time the paper prints. A local perspective is the only thing that might keep the reader's interest.

SAVE THE WORLD, BUT SAVE OUR LOOS FIRST!

But a local paper can report local news in lots of detail, because the readers will be interested in reading it.

QUEEN SAYS . . . "HAPPY BIRTHDAY" TO 115 YEAR-OLD HARRY MEEK, OF WHITE LODGE NURSING HOME

If a story has only local interest, it seldom makes it to the national papers (or to TV) unless there is something very unusual or amusing about it.

only a MENTION in the national paper and he's 115! Harry'll be on the warpath again.

'Cloned Pitbull Seen On Moon'

There's also the 'reporting' of events which probably didn't actually happen. Some newspapers specialise in wild and unlikely stories, such as '700,000 Cabbage Patch dolls recalled after kids nibbled by them' (*The National Enquirer*, USA) and '5-inch killer whale ate my Christmas turkey' (*The Sunday Sport*, UK). Maybe they shouldn't be called **news**papers . . .

700,000 CABBAGE PATCH DOLLS RECALLED AFTER KIDS NIBBLED BY THEM

5 INCH KILLER WHALE ATE MY CHRISTMAS TURKEY

How new is the news?

Newspaper printing deadlines have always affected what the papers could include in their editions. Morning papers in particular have critical distribution timetables, and if printing is late, they will miss out on sales. On the other hand, a newspaper which doesn't carry an important story won't be as popular as one that has managed to include it.

STOP PRESS STOP PRESS

When King George V died in 1936, the announcement of his death was delayed for several hours so that the 'respectable' morning newspapers would be first with the news, instead of the more sensational evening papers.

20 years ago, news programmes were much less frequent than they are today. People could only watch TV news and listen to radio news at fixed times of day. It didn't matter whether the news story happened at 10.00 am or 3.00 pm, if the bulletin was scheduled for 6.00 pm, you still had to wait until then to hear about it. It was only if something really momentous happened in between the regular scheduled news bulletins that other programmes were interrupted with a special report.

Today, news programming is very different. There are radio and TV stations that present news 24 hours a day, so you can catch the news when it's convenient for you, or follow a story as it develops, if it interests you. Those stations can present an ever-changing, in-depth account of a story, in a way that a daily – or even an hourly – news bulletin can never do.

..and now his left foot is coming up –
he's moving it forward as well...
this is very exciting, he's walking!
And there goes his right foot again..

There are news websites on the Internet, where you can follow a news story as it develops, explore alternative interpretations of news events, and discuss aspects of them with other Net users. You can fax or e-mail friends in other countries, too, to get their 'take' on one of their country's news stories before your own news programmes carry it, or hear their country's interpretation of a British story before it is discussed on our TV and radio.

When the Princess of Wales was killed very early in the morning in Paris, the British media had already closed down for the night. It was from friends in the United States and Australia that many people in Britain first heard news of the car crash, before their own news services resumed broadcasting the next morning.

Today, we have more access to national and international news than our parents and grandparents could ever have imagined. Sophisticated and vast news networks get important stories to every news programme in the world, in a matter of minutes. If you watch TV news you can hear reports of events which have happened within the last hour, or you can watch a live satellite broadcast from the other side of the world, and see the news as it happens.

This all makes the job of newspapers ever more difficult, for no medium such as a newspaper that prints once a day can possibly compete with 24-hour TV coverage that's always available. 'Late-breaking' news now belongs to TV, radio and the Internet, and many people believe that newspapers will have to change a lot to survive in the modern communications world (see page 112).

STOP PRESS STOP PRESS

Even some newspapers seem to think the days of printed news are over. *The Dallas Morning News* published an exclusive scoop about the Oklahoma City Bomber – but they put it on the Internet, not in their paper.

But the news media are not our only source of news information and comment.

Forms of popular culture such as cartoons and TV soaps, together with people like comedians and song-writers, all give us their own interpretation of current events.

Reading the meaning

If you had spent your whole life away from the influences of the modern media and had never watched TV or seen a film, you would find it almost impossible to follow what was happening on the TV screen.

The two-dimensional pictures we see every day
represent our three-dimensional world in a way
our eyes and brains have grown accustomed to.
The techniques used to tell a story use lots
of short-cuts which form a sort of visual shorthand
you'd have a lot of difficulty in explaining to an
outsider. Yet no one has ever sat down with you
and explained how to watch TV; it's just
something you have picked up from doing it.

mama

Reading the visual language of moving film is essential to our lives. But it means that we make assumptions automatically, without even being aware of them.

This is just some of the 'missing' information we fill in when we watch moving film. In fact, you can probably think of many more extra stages in between the pictures.
But no film maker can put them all into their film.
It would take a lifetime to show it!

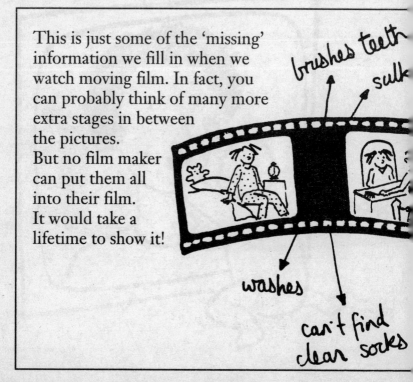

brushes teeth

sulk

washes

can't find clean socks

For example, in these pictures, we have learned to fill in the missing information that we need to make sense of the sequence of events in the 'story' that the pictures tell.

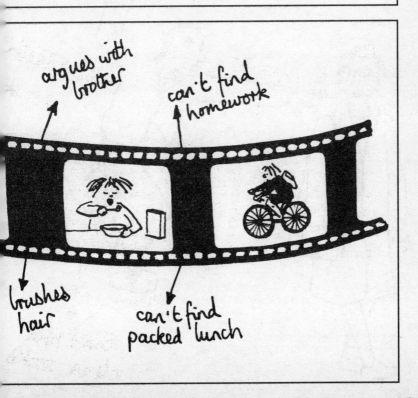

We all make assumptions about the material we see on TV and in movies. The people who make the programmes often anticipate our assumptions, and rely on them to help tell their story.

Or they may turn the expected assumptions upside down to challenge or confuse the audience. For example, this picture is based on a recent newspaper advertisement. Have a look at it, and decide what you think is happening.

The assumption that you probably made when you didn't see all of the picture, was that the young man was attacking the woman. Now, with more information, you can see that he was actually trying to save her life.

falling scaffolding

Camera angles

The use of different camera angles can also affect how you 'read' what you see on film, or even in a still photo. If you watch a TV news story about a conflict – for instance between the police and a group of demonstrators – it makes a big difference whether the film is shot from behind the police ...

... or behind the demonstrators.

It's easy to see only one side of the story.

The same thing is true if you watch a celebrity being pursued by photographers. You usually see the celebrity through the lens of one of the photographers.

But have you ever seen the encounter from the celebrity's viewpoint?

The banks of cameras flashing, and photographers calling out comments and questions and requests, has a very different effect.

The hero's point of view

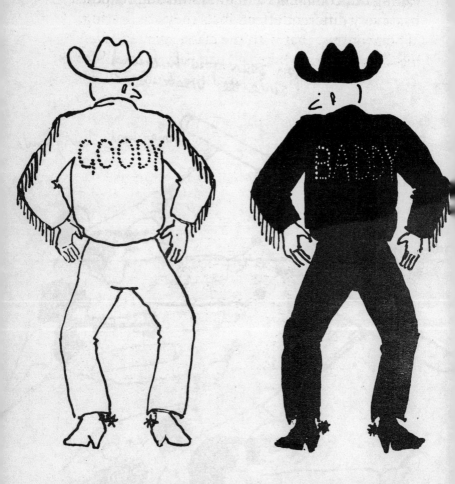

When you watch a TV drama or a film, you often get to see the action from a particular point of view: that of the hero or heroine. The story is told from their perspective and the camera looks at events through their eyes. Their thoughts and feelings, and their beliefs and needs, are what move the story forward.

For instance, think of a serious TV drama like *The Bill* – the point of view is always that of the police, and never that of the criminals they are chasing. Then contrast that with the classic comedy *Only Fools and Horses*, where the perspective is still from the hero's point of view – but this time, the hero is a petty criminal.

In both cases we end up liking the main characters – whether they're 'good' or 'bad' – because they're the characters we're told the most about and the characters we're given the most to identify with. We don't generally stop to try to see things from the other characters' points of view.

Even news items are often presented from only one point of view. We tend to think the news is unbiased – or that it should be. But the news often presents only one aspect of a story, or allows one aspect of a story to dominate.

The voice-over which accompanies film of an event might 'tell us what to think' about what we see. The people interviewed might be asked only particular questions, or the film might be edited to include only one sort of answer.

and that can go
and that can go
and that can go

Really, the news from a TV station is a product being offered for sale like any other commercial product. It is shaped and edited to appeal to certain viewers. If audiences like it, they'll continue to watch it. If they don't like the product, viewing figures fall. Commercial stations would then run the risk of going bust because advertisers would stop buying air-space from them. And the BBC wouldn't be able to justify supporting itself through charging people a licence fee.

Media stereotypes

A stereotype was originally a solid metal printing plate that had taken an impression and could reprint the same impression over and over again.

A stereotype was originally a solid metal printing plate that had taken an impression and could reprint the same impression over and over again.

A stereotype was originally a solid metal printing plate that had taken an impression and could reprint the same impression over and over again.

A **stereotype** represents someone as having certain set characteristics, rather than being an individual. You can see lots of examples of stereotyped characters in TV or radio soaps. They emphasise the predictable, so encouraging the viewer or reader to rely on judgements they have already made – their prejudices.

Old people who are
narrow-minded,
suspicious of any changes,
and wary of young people.

A successful business
woman who is cold,
unemotional and unattractive.

Country people who are
naive and foolish, and are
easily outwitted by smarter
city folk.

Americans who are brash,
demanding and loud-mouthed.

Fat people who are
jolly and noisy.

The list could go on and on.

Have another look at the two illustrations on pages
68 and 69. Are the assumptions that you made about
this character based on prejudice and stereotyping?

Stereotypes are one of the most pervasive aspects of human thinking. Young people are very often stereotyped in the media. You'll find lots of examples in TV dramas: of rebellious teenagers at odds with their parents or with society; of violent skinhead lager-louts with tattoos; of mean-minded or stupid punks with nose, eye-brow and belly-button rings . . .

But are people in real life as they often seem to be on the TV?

Many people think that stereotypes in the media increase prejudice in society, so stereotypes about race, sexual orientation and religious affiliation are especially worrying. Media propaganda in Nazi Germany certainly helped to spread the evil Nazi propaganda about Jews, and so helped to encourage violence against them.

If you see stereotyping in the media which you find offensive, you can complain about it. Check the reference section at the back of this book for details.

Controlling the media

Can the media say anything it likes? Can it tell lies about people, and get away with it? Can it investigate people's private lives without the people concerned being able to stop the intrusion?

In Britain, the Radio Authority was established in 1991 to license commercial radio stations. The Authority can regulate the material radio stations use – including their advertising. So material that some people would consider obscene or offensive cannot be used – or at least, not without running the risk of complaints. And the Authority can criticise, fine or take away the licences of stations that don't stick to the established code of practice.

In 1996 the Radio Authority received 624 complaints, and upheld 48 programming complaints and 87 advertising complaints. Fines were imposed on nine stations, either for breaching individual performance promises or one of the Radio Authority's codes.

In 1991 the Press Complaints Commission was set up to control and regulate the British press. And a new Code of Conduct for journalists came into force in Britain in January 1998. The tightest new aspects of the Code cover privacy, harassment, treatment of children, and intrusion into grief. It says . . .

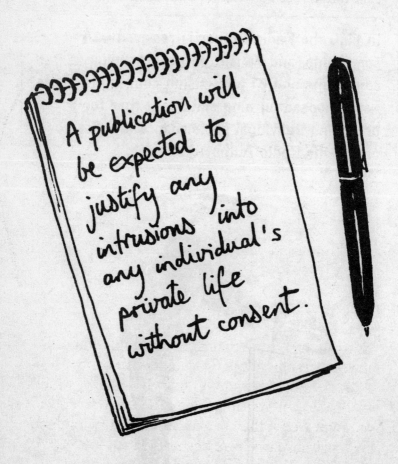

No one yet knows how effective the new code will be. Anyone can complain to the PCC about a story in a newspaper. The PCC will then investigate the complaint and make a judgement, which the newspaper in question is expected to print. However, the PCC cannot fine or close down a newspaper that breaks the Code of Conduct.

Many people think that this self-regulation of newspapers doesn't produce effective control. They believe there should be privacy laws, which would allow newspapers could be taken to court and punished if they broke the Code of Conduct. Such privacy laws have been discussed for many years, but have not yet been presented to Parliament.

A right to privacy?

At the end of 1997 the debate in Britain about the media's invasion of privacy grew very heated. Newspaper editors argued on TV and accused each other of lying and hypocrisy, and just about every channel of communication in the country took up the debate in some way.

your newspaper used the photos

So did your news programme

The cause of all this was, of course, the death of Diana, Princess of Wales, in a car crash.

At first, the media was literally blamed for Diana's death, for the accident seemed to have been caused by when she was fleeing from a group of paparazzi on motorbikes and in cars. Even later, when it was clear that this was not the only – or even the main, or immediate – cause of death, the debate and accusations continued.

Paparazzi are freelance photographers who follow celebrities around, trying to get intimate photos which they can then sell to newspapers. (The word 'paparazzi' comes from an Italian film, *La Dolce Vita*. One character – a sleazy photographer – was called Paparazzo.) In the years before the Princess of Wales' death, tabloid newspapers increasingly employed freelance photographers to trail and photograph her in private situations. In this way, the newspapers could truthfully deny that their own staff were responsible for any breaches of privacy.

The issues involved in the debates about the media's invasion of privacy are not always straightforward ones. Here is just a sample of the opinions which feed the debate.

If people didn't buy the papers that print these lying stories and invasive pictures, then newspapers wouldn't print them. It's the buying public's fault, not the newspapers.

It's hypocritical to put all the blame on the red-top tabloids. The so-called respectable newspapers just wait for the tabloid stories to hit the streets, and then they reprint them. They often use all the same invasive details.

Diana was hounded to death by all the media attention she received. She tried to turn the interest into good by her charity work, but in the end she lost the battle.

Diana manipulated the media herself, and often tried to influence and alter the stories the newspapers carried about her. She even gave a TV interview herself, with lots of very private details about her life. She invited and encouraged the attention.

If you had any idea of what it's like to be hassled by 30 or 40 journalists for hours or even days, at a time, and followed everywhere by them, you'd know how dreadful it makes you feel. Wouldn't you try to manipulate them too, and turn the attention into something more positive? Isn't that sort of manipulation just good public relations?

Self-regulation of the press by the press will never be effective. Even the new Code of Conduct is too hard to define, and so too difficult to put into practice. The media should be responsible in law for the actions it takes.

Any person in the public eye also has a private life. Many people argue that public figures should only be the object of media attention whilst they carry out their public duties. The media attention, they say, shouldn't spill over into the private lives of public people. Everyone, they believe, should be allowed to be private with their families and friends, without having to worry about being photographed or followed.

But other people say that just can't happen. They think it's often too hard to separate public life from private, and that in any case, if public figures have scandalous private lives, it is in the public interest for that to be exposed.

Of course, it's true that any public figure who does something illegal in their private life wants to try to keep that hidden. And any good investigative journalist will try to uncover those secrets. But many people support a law that would protect the private life of public figures unless their private actions affect the general public.

The media have often revealed uncomfortable truths that public figures would rather have kept secret. And sometimes, the uncovering of secrets has been very much in the public interest.

The Watergate campaign in America, for instance, revealed a series of illegal actions on the part of a special committee of people who reported to the President, Richard Nixon. The newspaper which investigated the story, *The Washington Post*, took a big risk in publishing the story as it unfolded. It was threatened with legal action by the President's office, but it persisted and the revelations were important ones.

Media intrusion, harassment and intimidation can and do happen when a 'hot' story is being chased. But it is easy to think of media campaigns which have been forces for good.

Live Aid was heavily publicised and promoted in newspapers and on TV, and it helped to save many lives as well as alter people's thinking about the issues of famine. The same is true of the campaign to ban landmines. And if you have a local issue that needs publicity, nothing will work better for you than a media campaign.

'Everyone has the right to respect for his private and family life, his home and his correspondence.'

Article Eight,
European Convention on
Human Rights

Censored!

The media are such a central part of any country's communications, that all governments exert control over them to some extent. For example, in Britain, the government controls the licensing of the air waves, and of commercial TV companies as well. They can even withhold top-secret information from the public by means of a D (for Defence) notice. This can be used, for example, to prevent British spies being named, or their photos published.

Even in recent years, many books have been banned in libraries and classrooms. The most frequently banned books in the 1990s in the USA include: <u>The Chocolate War</u> by Robert Cormier, <u>Scary Stories In The Dark</u> by Alvin Schwartz, <u>The Witches</u> by Roald Dahl, <u>Forever</u> by Judy Blume, <u>In The Night Kitchen</u> by Maurice Sendak, and <u>Little Red Riding Hood</u>, by the Grimm Brothers.

In some countries, effective censorship is relatively easy. If you control your own country's media, prevent foreign books, newspapers and magazines from entering the country, and can block or deflect foreign TV and radio broadcasts from being picked up, you can do a good job of preventing people from knowing what is really happening. You can make sure they are told lies, or not told anything at all.

But, even then, many ordinary people will understand very well that the media are controlled and will find out information in some other way. And today, there is an excellent way of doing that, which is very difficult to censor or to control – the Internet.

The Internet is an international electronic communication network which is widely expected to lead the communications revolution of the next century. It became available commercially in 1994, and if you have a computer and a telephone line you can get access to it and link up to a bewildering range of information and entertainment. Already in Britain 5% of households are connected to it. (In London, 21% of PC owners are wired up.) You can send and receive electronic mail around the world in a few seconds, and you can browse through millions of **websites** established by governments, commercial companies and individuals. It is almost impossible to censor the Internet effectively. And, because it is not affected by international borders, and is mostly fed by contributions from individuals, it is also extremely hard to monitor and police it.

Some controls have already been imposed on the Internet in America, but no one yet knows if the controls can be effective. The US government has introduced legislation to limit what people put on the Net, especially indecent or pornographic material. In Singapore, the government is trying to restrict the sites that people can access, through its licensing of the 'browser' software that can be installed in computers.

you're under arrest

Sex and violence

How much violence do you watch on TV?
Do you think it matters if you watch violent
shows? Do your parents try to stop you from
watching late-night programmes or age-restricted
films and videos?

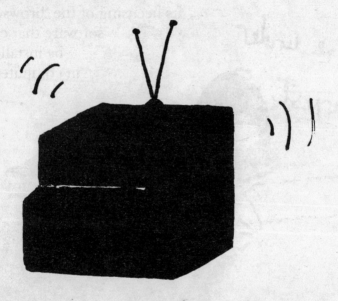

There have been more than 3,000 studies of TV
violence since the 1950s and all of them seem to
agree that heavy watchers of violent TV are more
aggressive than light watchers. The average
American child will have watched 100,000 acts of
media violence by the time they finish elementary
school, around the age of 12. American children
watch more TV than British kids, and most have a
wider range of channels to choose from. But even
if British children watch just half that, it's still an
awful lot.

When it comes to sex in the media, the kind of sex you can watch these days on British TV depends on the channel you watch, and the time you watch it. Terrestrial TV channels in Britain leave out 'adult' sex scenes and heavy swearing until after 9 pm, when young children are expected to be in bed. However, satellite and cable channels broadcast all over the world in different time zones, so they don't observe any time constraints.

Should the amount of sex and violence on TV be controlled? Many people think so. One group of parents in America are so concerned they have demanded the use of a device called a V-chip (V stands for viewer-control, or veto, as well as for violence) to prevent their children from watching certain programmes on the TV sets in their homes.

move Dad

According to a new law in the USA (and a similar law in Canada) the makers of TV sets have to build in a device that will block out certain programmes according to their ratings. Parents can choose the kinds of violence they will allow their children to see, and each network will have to send out coded information before each programme goes on air. (This is especially useful if young children watch TV in their own bedrooms, when their parents don't necessarily know what they are watching.)

But what about real-life violence on news programmes, like war footage – should that also be controlled? And what about people who don't find the level of violence offensive – should their watching habits be censored by others? And what about music CDs? And videos? The possible influences, for good and bad, are almost boundless – especially with the Internet available.

The big business of mass media

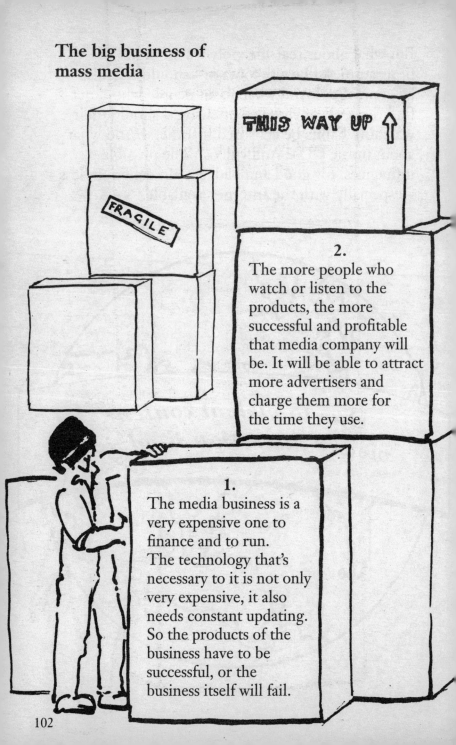

FRAGILE

THIS WAY UP ⇧

2.
The more people who watch or listen to the products, the more successful and profitable that media company will be. It will be able to attract more advertisers and charge them more for the time they use.

1.
The media business is a very expensive one to finance and to run. The technology that's necessary to it is not only very expensive, it also needs constant updating. So the products of the business have to be successful, or the business itself will fail.

3.

Like any other modern public company, a media company depends on profits. (The only exception is the BBC, which is funded by its licence fees.

Although the BBC is still expected to help fund itself from the sale of programmes overseas, and from the sale of programme-related books, videos and so forth, this income represents only about 5% of its running costs.)

FRAGILE

The business interests – News Corp.

Rupert Murdoch's News Corporation is one of the most powerful media empires in the world, and made US $9 billion in 1995. Here are some of the businesses that it owns:

AUSTRALIA
Adelaide
newspapers: *Adelaide Advertiser, Mercury, Sunday Mail*
Melbourne
Ansett Airlines
Computer Power
newspapers: *Herald-Sun, Sunday Herald-Sun, Northern Territory News*
Perth
newspapers: *Sunday Times, Sunday Mail*
Sydney (News Corporation Headquarters)
newspapers: *The Australian, Daily Telegraph Mirror, Sunday Telegraph, Cumberland Newspapers*
TV Week (magazine)
Ansett Worldwide Aviation Services
Seven Television Network
Festival Records

BRITAIN
newspapers: *The Sun, The Times, News of the World, The Sunday Times, Today*
HarperCollins U.K. (publisher)
BSkyB & Sky News (TV channel)
News Datacom (technology)

ITALY
Prego! (TV networks and advertising)

GERMANY
Vox (TV channel)

HONG KONG
Star TV
Star Movies
Star Radio
JSkyB (TV channel)
Golden Harvest & Golden Princess (movie libraries)
AsiaSat2 (satellite)
Pacific Magazines and Printing Limited
TV Asahi

NEW ZEALAND
Independent Newspapers

SOUTH AMERICA
Canal Fox (TV)

INDIA
Zee TV

AMERICA	ASkyB (TV channel)
Chicago	Echostar Alliance (500 Channels)
WFLD, Channel 32 (TV)	NYPD Blue (TV programme)
Dallas	World League Football
DKAF, Channel 33	News America FSI
Heritage Media	*New York Post* (newspaper)
Houston	A Current Affair
KRIV, Channel 26	The Weekly Standard
Los Angeles	*TV Guide* (magazine)
Twentieth Century Fox	New World Communications
Film Corporation	Group
Twentieth Century	fX
Fox Television	News Technology Group
Fox Broadcasting Company	Delphi Internet Services
24-hour Fox News Channel	HarperCollins (publisher)
Fox Video	**Salt Lake City**
Fox Interactive	KSTU, Channel 13 (TV)
Savoy Pictures Entertainment	**Washington D.C.**
New York City	*The Standard* (newspaper)
News Corp.'s US HQ	WTTG, Channel 5 (TV)
FOX & FOX News (TV stations)	MCI
WNYW, Channel 5 (TV)	

One of the reasons for concern about such global power is that it might affect reporting of news or opinions, because of possible damage to business interests in other parts of the empire. Some people think that this danger was demonstrated in 1998, when HarperCollins, a British publisher owned by News Corp., decided not to publish a book that was critical of the Chinese Government. Several commentators thought that this was to protect News Corp.'s TV interests in China, although HarperCollins maintained that this was not their reason for not publishing the book.

Calling all shoppers!

Advertising is crucial to commercial media companies. Without the money paid by advertisers, many companies wouldn't be able to afford to make TV programmes, play CDs, or publish newspapers and magazines. (Even the BBC, which doesn't carry advertisements from outside companies, still advertises its own products.)

And advertisers bring in a lot of money! For instance, in the USA it costs about $1 million a minute to run an advertisement during an episode of E.R.

Advertising is such an ordinary part of our media-inhabited lives that few people question its existence. Does it matter that TV and radio carry lots of commercials? Do you even notice them very much? Well, the advertisers think you do! You probably watch thousands of commercials on TV in a year, and they're just the regular ones slotted into commercial breaks.

SPOT THE PRODUCT PLACEMENT

There is also the 'hidden' advertising of **product placement** – if you see a well-known soft drink prominently displayed during a popular TV show or film, or see the characters wearing brand-name clothes, you can bet that the manufacturer has paid to have it shown in the programme. Next time you watch a TV soap, make a point of counting up the brand names you can see around.

Small is beautiful

At the opposite end of the scale to the big multi-national corporations, are small media organisations. Everything is different here! The technology is usually limited and the products are alternative and specialised, for a local audience.

Fanzines (magazines for fans) are a good example of this. In fact they're not entirely new. Versions of 'zines have been around since the early part of this century, when science-fiction fans, anarchists and poets exchanged their thoughts on duplicated pages.

And from the '50s through to the '70s, music and movie-star fans established underground communities, connected across the miles by their obscure publications.

Desk-top publishing helped 'zines to multiply in the '80s, and today they have become one of the latest hip phenomena. But, if 'zines become very successful they too may become mainstream, and lose their alternative audiences! The people who like the unconventional style of underground material will probably just move on to the next fanzine that becomes available.

THE FUTURE

The 20th century information revolution has transformed the ways in which we get access to information and communicate with other people. New forms of the media – like satellite TV, and the Internet – seem to be increasingly in popularity so fast that the older forms – like newspapers – have lost ground to them. Above all, the keyword for future development in communication channels seems to be: interactivity.

Don't just sit there and wait for the news to come to you – get out there and surf the Net!

Interactivity enables us to participate in the communication process in ways that were simply not possible even 20 years ago. Then, the newspaper was delivered to your door and you relied on it to tell you the news, and to help shape (or confirm) your opinions about that news. Then, 90% of American homes used to watch the evening news on TV. Now only 20% do, for they can instead choose to watch news programmes at a time to suit them on 24-hour cable news channels.

Will newspapers and conventional television survive into the 21st century? The answer is certainly 'yes'. But newspapers are already changing to incorporate many aspects of the more modern forms of media with which they increasingly must compete. Most newspapers now include more comment and more magazine-like information rather than just the news and news analysis, which other media now do better. Newspapers today are often designed to look more like magazines, and often incorporate interactive features such as e-mail addresses.

this is how we communicated vital information back in the 20th century

how PRIMITIVE

Audience interaction is a new, and powerful, direction for the media. Call-ins, phone-ins, phone polls, fax numbers, voice-mail lines all encourage it.

The on-line services of the digital new media also support this new trend. The users are constantly selecting from menus, getting news, exchanging e-mail, and meeting in virtual groups and chat rooms for discussions. These users have far more control over their media than any newspaper or magazine reader.

Talk radio literally depends on interaction – and from hundreds of stations in the USA in 1980 there are now thousands of them.

Confessional chat shows are now enormously popular on TV, both in America and Britain. No subject is too bizarre for these shows and they attract enormous audiences.

And so, in contrast to the old media's decline, interactive media's cable, talk radio, audience participation radio and TV shows, digital communities, websites, and <u>computer conferencing</u> systems are all on the increase.

There is now a vast mixture of formal and informal electronic communication networks available in the western world and increasingly, throughout the world. These encompass a range of technologies, like fax machines, telephones, broadcast and cable mass media, satellite and cellular communications, computer networks, and so on. Computer on-line services also offer their customers bulletin boards, magazine articles, researching and shopping facilities along with access to the Internet.

This all suggests the possibility of a major change in the way humans can communicate and use communication systems, and a lot more power in the hands of ordinary people.

However, there are problems related to this flood of new technology. Its advantages and power are still only available to the wealthy and privileged, and if that continues, the distinctions between rich and poor in tomorrow's world could be increased rather than diminished.

lots of people in the world don't even have electricity, never mind a TV

And there are practical problems too. For example, **cyber-terrorism** has become a genuine threat. (This is when thousands of computers linked to the Internet can be made to crash, or can be infected with electronic viruses.)

So what does the future look like? Well, it may not be very far away – and it probably looks a lot like this.

The machinery of the new media will soon be packaged and sold in simple, reliable formats. You'll buy something that looks very much like a TV, but it will have everything you need tucked inside it and all accessible with some sort of super-zapper or keyboard control.

You'll take it out of the box and plug it into an electric socket or a phone-jack, although advances in technology may also make even that unnecessary.

man's best friend?

The control will call up commercial and cable channels, home entertainment systems, e-mail, reference material, banking on-line services, movies and videos, shopping channels and website dictionaries (all things already in widespread use) using icons you'll just push or click on.

Upgrades, new products and extra software will all be transmitted and installed through fibre-optic lines coming into your house, or perhaps through cable modems.

This network will enable us to tele-commute to work. Some people do this already.

It will create ultra-accessible schools, with much better libraries and reference materials than any ordinary school could ever hope to have.

But remember, this is only a prediction about the future. We may be as far away from the truth as Alexander Bell was about the coming use of telephones when he invented them.

THE ONLY WAY TO KNOW FOR SURE ABOUT THE FUTURE IS TO WATCH IT HAPPEN!

HOW TO COMPLAIN ABOUT NEWSPAPERS AND MAGAZINES

To complain about **advertisements** in magazines and newspapers, write or phone the Advertising Standards Authority, 2 Torrington Place, London WC1E 7HW.
Tel 0171 580 5555 Fax 0171 323 4339.

To complain about the **content** or the **conduct** of magazines and newspapers, write or phone the Press Complaints Commission, 1 Salisbury Square, London EC4 8AE.
Tel 0171 353 1248 Fax 0171 353 8355.

HOW TO COMPLAIN ABOUT RADIO AND TELEVISION

The BBC - Telephone 0181 743 8000 to make TV comments and criticisms, or 0171 580 4468 to make radio comments and criticisms. The address to write to is BBC Viewer and Listener Correspondence, Villiers House, the Broadway, London W5 2PA.

ITV, Channel 4 and licensed cable or satellite TV - Write or phone the Independent Television Commission, 33 Foley Street, London W1P 7LB.
Tel 0171 255 3000 Fax 0171 306 7800.
The Broadcasting Standards Commission, 7 The Sanctuary, London SW1P 3JS
(Tel 0171 222 3172, Fax 0171 233 0544) can also be contacted to complain about a breach of

privacy, or unjust or unfair treatment on radio or television.

Radio - To complain about independent radio write or phone the Radio Authority, Holbrook House, 14 Great Queen Street, London WC2B 5DG. Tel 0171 430 2724 Fax 0171 405 7064.

General - You could contact the Department for Culture, Media & Sport, 2-4 Cockspur Street, London SW1Y 5DH - the government department responsible for the media - or your local Member of Parliament.

Tips for making effective complaints

1. Write as soon as possible after seeing or hearing the programme or advertisement.

2. Be as specific as possible about your complaint.

3. Be very polite, but be firm and clear about the points you want to make.

4. Ask for an answer.

5. Keep a copy of your letter or fax, and keep notes about any phone calls.

6. Consider writing direct to the producer of the programme - if you want to raise just a small point, this might work better, and more quickly, than the official channels listed above.

USEFUL READING

The best media reference book is probably
The Media Guide, produced each year by *The
Guardian* newspaper and published by Fourth
Estate. Any local library with a reference section
should have a recent copy of it. This handbook is
jam-packed with facts and figures about all aspects
of the media in Britain.

An excellent way to find out more about the media
is to study examples of it. You could even set up a
media-monitoring project yourself. Choose a
topic that interests you, and keep notes on the
number of times it is mentioned over a period of
time - say, a week. Ask yourself these questions, to
get started.

How much coverage does your issue get?

What are the sources for the stories, listed or
mentioned in the coverage?

Where did each story come from? Did a reporter
go out to cover it, or did the newspaper, radio or
TV company use another source?

Is the coverage of your issue factual, or is it based
on opinion?

Do all the stories agree about the facts, or do they
say different things?

CHILDREN'S EXPRESS - a young people's news agency

This organisation is part news agency, part youth club, and has members between 8 and 18 years of age, who aim to reach policy-makers by getting their views into the media. The programme operates in two tiers. Younger children, aged 8 to 13, are the reporters, and are trained by the older children, aged 14 to 18, who also take responsibility for editing and overseeing the editorial activities. The young people run the reporters' board and editors' board, determine which stories to follow, initiate research and interviews, and work together in teams to realise their aims. The stories cover a range of issues from how easy it is to buy a lottery ticket if you are under 16, or the impact of rising drug abuse on their lives, to how the media stereotype young people.

At present, you can only participate in person if you live close by one of the two bureaux (in London and Newcastle) although more bureaux are planned. But if you have access to the Internet you can log on to their website and participate virtually instead!

Contact Rowena Young, the Bureau Chief, Children's Express, Exmouth House, 3-11 Pine Street, London EC1R 0JH.
Tel 0171 833 2577 Fax 1071 278 7722
Email cexpres@ibm.net

WEBSITES

If you have access to the Internet, you'll find some sites called **ezines**, which is short for electronic magazines. Just like paper magazines, these have great features to read, but there are also interactive things to do. Their pages change frequently – sometimes more than once a month. Here are some to try.

Little Planet Times
http://littleplanettimes.com/
This is a newspaper for young people, by young people.

Pathfinder – Time For Kids
http://www.pathfinder.com/@@1XMV
agUALRnUno@n/TFK/
This is an American news service for young people.

Yakity Yak
http://www.myfavoriteco.com/zeen.html
This is a chatty ezine with great characters.

Too Cool For Grown-Ups
http://www.tcfg.com/
This is an ezine about the Web itself. It will take you all over the Net, and you can even cast your vote for the Top Ten Websites.

GLOSSARY

advertorial an advertising feature in a magazine or newspaper, written to look and sound like part of the regular editorial material.

analogue transmissions for radio and TV are received in the same form in which they are sent, using variations in sine waves. Most standard telephone lines in the world are analogue ones.

broadsheets large-format British newspapers that are generally serious in their coverage of news.

cable TV TV that is transmitted to the set through a cable link into your home.

censorship The government control of public information by restricting what broadcasting and publishing companies can say or have access to.

commercial sector media paid for by advertising, such as Channel 4 TV.

computer conferencing an electronic way of 'meeting' with long-distance work colleagues or clients through connected computer systems.

digital transmissions for radio and TV are sent as a series of on and off electrical pulses – the pictures and sounds are coded as a string of binary digits (that is, a series of ones and noughts). This is sharper and more accurate than analogue transmissions.

fanzines magazines for fans of a particular interest – e.g. specialist sports and music interests.

interactive an entertainment system which relies on the active participation of the viewer or listener.

media the collection of communication channels in the modern world - e.g. TV, radio, newspapers, etc.

moveable type where single letters were produced and assembled into pages of text ready to be printed. The pages could then be broken down and re-assembled to make new text. This invention revolutionised printing techniques. Electronic techniques are now used instead.

paparazzi freelance photographers who follow celebrities around in the hope of getting a good shot to sell to newspapers and magazines.

product placement a form of advertising, in which companies pay to have their products on display in popular forms of the media, such as TV soaps.

public sector media paid for by public money (licence fees or taxes). The BBC is funded largely from licence fees.

satellite TV TV that is transmitted to your set from a series of satellite links. You need to install a dish to receive the signals.

sound-bite a quick summary of someone's opinion, in a few words or a brief sentence.

spin doctor a professional public relations expert employed by an organisation to try to turn news stories to the organisation's advantage.

stereotype the representation of a person as a predictable representative of a certain group or 'type', rather than an individual.

terrestrial TV TV that is transmitted to your set from 'earth-based' sources, rather than satellite or cable ones.

tabloids small-format British newspapers that tend to focus on sensational news stories, rather than serious ones.

website a point of information on the World Wide Web, which is part of the Internet. It is estimated that there are about two million websites available at present, established by individuals, organisations and companies to advertise their products and services, and offer information and entertainment.

INDEX

oral tradition of storytelling 27

WHAT'S THE BIG IDEA?

Have you read them all?

0 340 722630	Alien Life	£3.99	☐
0 340 667206	Animal Rights	£3.99	☐
0 340 67847X	The Environment	£3.99	☐
0 340 724056	Food*	£3.99	☐
0 340 708778	Genetics	£3.99	☐
0 340 722916	The Media	£3.99	☐
0 340 655887	The Mind	£3.99	☐
0 340 693398	Nuclear Power	£3.99	☐
0 340 714824	The Paranormal*	£3.99	☐
0 340 667192	Religion	£3.99	☐
0 340 655909	Time and the Universe	£3.99	☐
0 340 655917	Virtual Reality	£3.99	☐
0 340 655895	Women's Rights	£3.99	☐

* coming soon

Turn the page to find out how to order these books.

ORDER FORM

Books in this series are available at your local bookshop, or can be ordered direct from the publisher. A complete list of titles is given on the previous page. Just tick the titles you would like and complete the details below. Prices and availability are subject to change without prior notice.

Please enclose a cheque or postal order made payable to Bookpoint Ltd, and send to: Hodder Children's Books, Cash Sales Dept, Bookpoint, 39 Milton Park, Abingdon, Oxon OX14 4TD.
Email address: orders@bookpoint.co.uk.

If you would prefer to pay by credit card, our call centre team would be delighted to take your order by telephone. Our direct line is 01235 400414 (lines open 9.00 am – 6.00 pm, Monday to Saturday; 24 hour message answering service). Alternatively you can send a fax on 01235 400454.

Title .... First name .... Surname ....

Address ....

....

....

Daytime tel .... Postcode ....

If you would prefer to post a credit card order, please complete the following.

Please debit my Visa/Access/Diners Card/American Express (delete as applicable) card number:

Signature .... Expiry Date ....

If you would NOT like to receive further information on our products, please tick ☐

128